# SELF-PUBLISHING FAST TRACK

*7 Easy Steps to Write Your
First Book and Share Your Story*

**JENELLE JACK**

# Table of Contents

# Self-Publishing with Purpose

# CHAPTER 1

## READY TO SPREAD YOUR MESSAGE

There are thousands of people who dream of publishing their own book. But so many potential authors never set their ideas down on paper. Instead, these jewels remain stuck instead their heads like unearthed diamonds. Why? Most of these would-be authors lack confidence in their ability to write well, or are anxious about being judged by others, or they lack the commitment necessary to write their book.

These same people witness new books being published all the time. They check out the Amazon bestseller lists, they hear about the housewife, the accountant, or the school teacher who was recently published, and they see the book ads in the magazines they leaf through.

Take it from someone who's been there. Today, I have an M.A. in Writing from Johns Hopkins University, but before I decided to invest in myself and study the craft of writing—before I went on to self-publish my own books—I had doubt.

But let me make this clear: You don't need a degree to pursue writing. What I've discovered is that one factor tends to separate those who write and publish their book from those who let it remain a dream—or, if they've written a draft, let it end up tucked away inside a drawer.

That factor is belief.

Confidence is what allows people to get anything done, and the writing process is no different.

And what about those people who do write and hit the publish button?

They've done it knowing they're no Hemingway, yet they had something valuable to say. Writing isn't about leaving people in awe over your sentence structure.

It's about delivering something valuable or entertaining to the reader, and doing so with clarity. A reader should finish your book feeling that their time was well spent.

The main thing you'll realize, once you start the writing process and your words fill up the page, is that it can be done.

Perhaps you want to self-publish a book because you have a business. You know that books lend to a brand's credibility, that they've helped business owners establish their expertise, and that they've enabled many people to garner speaking opportunities.

Writing a book takes time, but it's worth it. By self-publishing, you'll automatically distinguish yourself from your peers as someone knowledgeable about your subject, and as a person who can provide your clients with value.

Or maybe, once you've finished reading this book, you'll want to write fiction. But as a professional who's always had a desire to write a novel, somewhere in the back of your mind is the thought that fiction is nonessential.

After all, novels aren't business books.

They don't teach people how to make money, or how to take care of their health, or how to improve their relationships.

But let me tell you: many works of fiction have changed the course of entire lives. They've emboldened readers to find the strength to leave an undesirable situation, travel the world, gain self-esteem, or simply to imagine more deeply.

And there are thousands of authors who started with one fiction book, then wrote another, and another. Who watched their book sales snowball, and soon enough found their desire to quit their job becoming a possibility.

Whether your goal is to write nonfiction or fiction, if you have the desire to self-publish, this book will help you with that process. And once you've implemented what you learn, you'll have a clearer path to obtaining the success you want to achieve.

# CHAPTER 2

## REASONS TO SELF-PUBLISH NOW

I'm going to start from the top with why now's a good time to self-publish. First, by self-publishing, you'll have complete control over your creative process.

I wrote my first novel when I was in college, then spent months mailing off queries to literary agents. Back then, if you wanted your book to reach readers you had to go through the gatekeepers—literary agents and book publishers.

I got back rejection letters as well as requests for a partial or the full manuscript. But during this time, I stumbled upon an article about the growing self-publishing industry and I knew it was the right path for me.

Today, if you're willing to go the self-publishing route, literary agents are no longer necessary to getting your book into readers' hands. You as the writer are your own literary agent, and after your book is complete, it's up to you to choose an editor, cover designer, and book formatter. If you're a fast writer, you can spend a couple weeks writing and have your book in the hands of readers in less than 90 days.

The second reason why now's a good time to self-publish is marketing.

Traditionally published authors have to fit into one of three categories: be a bestselling author, have links to a well-known brand, or have a large platform in order to get a marketing push. And that's if you're lucky.

There are many authors who sell thousands of books and still are tasked with creating their own marketing plan. If you're a midlist author, you can forget about a traditional publisher getting behind you.

So here's the thing: if you have to market your book for yourself anyway, the self-publishing route just makes more sense. After all, you know the strengths of your book. There are many avenues to marketing your book, including book newsletters, Amazon ads, author swaps, blog tours, and podcasts.

The third reason to self-publish is economics. Do it yourself, and you'll be better compensated.

Traditional publishers send authors their royalty statements at set intervals throughout the year. Part of their sales process includes shipping the hardcover or paperback format of an author's book to bookstores. But if no one buys it, those books are sent back to them.

Because there's no way to estimate your sales ahead of time, and you were probably given an advance payment as a traditionally published author, this will be viewed as a major loss for them. Lackluster sales even lead most publishers to drop authors after their first book.

There are many self-published writers who once had a traditional contract. If a publisher gives you an advance and you didn't sell as many books as expected, know that it's the only time you will be published by them. They will drop you because you didn't fulfill the contract by selling sufficient books to cover the costs of your advance.

As a self-published author, you can check your sales every single day if you choose, as sales numbers are updated almost in real time. You'll never be in limbo about what your sales numbers look like. Not only that, your royalty percentage will be higher.

Right now, if you publish on Amazon and set your book to $0.99—which is the lowest it can be—your royalties would be $0.35 per book.

If you price your book at $2.99 or more, your royalties would be 70% per book. Barnes & Noble, along with other platforms, have a comparable system.

The fourth reason now's a good time to self-publish is you can edit or revise your book whenever you want.

Let's say you publish your book, decide to read it again, and you find errors. This does happen, though I'll advise you to avoid this by proofreading your book and having it professionally edited.

But let's say you find misspelled words, or you called a character by the wrong name in a certain chapter, or you've named the wrong mountain, and so on. As a self-published author, you have the power to edit your manuscript at any time and re-upload it to an online book platform.

Platforms like Amazon, Barnes & Noble, and Draft2Digital allow authors to make edits whenever they want. You can even change your book cover. Especially as a first-time author, mistakes can happen. Perhaps you hadn't pinpointed your sub-genre and want a cover change to attract more potential readers. I know authors who have changed just their book cover and saw sales skyrocket.

Things like this can only be done if you self-publish and have control of the process. And contrary to the popular saying *not* to judge a book by its cover, in the self-publishing industry, people nearly always judge a book by its cover.

These are the four main reasons why now's a good time to self-publish. But best of all, by doing so you'll have peace of mind that the process is following your own timeline. You are the captain of your book's ship.

# CHAPTER 3

# YOUR STORY MATTERS

You may have wondered to yourself, "Does my story really matter?" I am here to tell you that it does.

Know this: you're not the first person to wonder if you should go through all the effort of writing your book. After all, you can spend weeks or months writing a book and not have many people read it.

On the other hand, you can spend weeks and months writing a book and have hundreds or even thousands of people read it.

Either way, you only had to do the work once.

Writing a book is an interesting process, because no one's really one hundred percent certain that they'll find success. But I'm going to share with you now why telling your story is important, and in a later chapter I'll help you with the process of getting those words out faster.

The length of time you might think you have to spend writing your book is probably much longer than if you have the right systems in place. Yes, I'm going to spill the tea on how you can probably write that book within 90 days. But before we talk about that, I have a question for you.

Why do you enjoy other people's stories?

I'm sure you've read at least a couple books outside of school. And whether it was because you wanted to learn a new skill or be entertained, you probably turned the pages because the author did a fine job weaving together the elements of storytelling. Even nonfiction books that readers reference over and over again include strongly woven elements of storytelling.

For instance, if you were writing a book about job hunting, you wouldn't just give people the cut-and-dry details, like how to craft your resume, format a cover letter, find potential employers, and so on.

You'd include stories about other people's job searching experiences and share what worked for them. You'd tell your readers their names, the types of companies they got jobs with, and what worked and didn't work in their job hunting endeavors.

And what will readers recall the best? A few facts that they believe will be most helpful to them, and...the stories. Why? Stories are easy to recall. It'll be easier for the readers of this book to recall what they need to do to transition into the working world because of the stories involved.

My point is, you took the time to read someone else's book because you either wanted to learn something, or you wanted to be entertained. And you believed that author had a story to tell, that his or her experience was worth sharing. And chances are you neither knew nor met this author, but you committed to spending time with them by reading their book.

So why wouldn't you believe that once you're delivering something of value, whether it's education or entertainment, there will be someone on the other end who wants to read your book?

What makes you think someone isn't out there waiting to be helped by your story, isn't going to have an *aha!* moment because of your experience, or wouldn't be entertained by the world you've created with your words?

**As long as you have something valuable to offer another person, you must throw off the cloak of doubt.** Believe in yourself, because one thing is certain: you must be confident in the project you're about to create. Confidence is what will push you through.

What's that? Your confidence is kind of shaky? Do you feel that another person's story is more valid than your own?

The reason for this second struggle is that many people get stuck on the comparison train. And guess what? This train doesn't really have a destination. Instead, it goes around and around in circles unless you hop off.

Stay on the train and you'll end up doing things like looking at what other authors have done and freezing up at the thought of writing.

You wouldn't see the other side of things—that even bestsellers didn't just spring from a writer's mind in their final form. No, there was a first draft, and maybe a second and a third. All books have to be edited. Know that your story is valid.

There's a group of readers out there who won't get a concept until you explain it from your point of view.

Why? Because your voice will be the one that cuts through the noise.

Have you ever heard of an author's "voice?" This terminology is used because an author's personality often comes through on the page. This is why there can be two books on the same topic—let's say, the Paleo diet—and two different types of readers are attracted to each one.

Who needs to read your story?

Self-publishing is like any other industry, and representation matters. I love getting books at the library for my son whose characters on the cover and inside the story reflect little brown boys. Yes, we can enjoy reading any book we find interesting, but when we start reading a book and there's something about what the author has created that we can identify with— whether it's because one of the characters is a female, a chef, a single mother, a high-school dropout, Indian, Asian, African-American, and so on—it matters.

There are so many stories and so many experiences in this world that go unheard.

But you have the privilege of living in a time when, if you want your voice to be heard, you can make the decision to put in the work and hit the publish button. Now's a good time to put your story out onto the market. The visibility you'll receive can open up new opportunities, including access to author events, consulting, and media appearances. Your book will precede you when it comes to gaining new opportunities.

If no one is trying to silence you, then why are you muting your own voice?

Whose life can you change by sharing a story, starting with your own?

Your story has a place and is just as significant as the next person's. It's time for you to share it.

Really, an idea for a book is much like any other idea. Will you bring your idea to life, potentially changing your own life and impacting others' lives? Or you will let it stay inside you? Who is missing out on being entertained by the tales in your head? Who is missing out on learning something so helpful, it could have a significant, long-term effect on their family's life?

The good thing for the world is that, as with any other idea that lays dormant, someone else may quite possibly have it, and they will act. Don't let that be you—the person who watches someone else execute your idea.

Today, you have the ability to write your book and the opportunity to publish from the comfort of your own home. Your book can reach the masses.

In the self-publishing industry, thousands of books are being published every month, and it's becoming more challenging for a book to rise to the top. This is even more reason to start your journey and share your story.

Begin now and your learning process, should you choose to write more than one book, will be so much easier all because you started your publishing journey.

My last question is, what are you willing to do in order to share your story in a book?

If you weren't willing to share your story, you wouldn't be reading this book. So I encourage you to move forward with your idea. In the next few chapters, I'm going to help make this writing thing an easier process for you. Show up for yourself, fake discipline (if you have to) until it becomes something real, and strive for consistency.

If you choose to write consistently, you'll be able to build momentum, which will both encourage you and propel you toward a finished product. But before you can really dive into any of this writing stuff, you have to start with one core truth: your story matters.

# CHAPTER 4

# BEFORE YOU WRITE YOUR BOOK

Here are three things you should do before writing a book.

Every week, thousands of books are published. Today, there are several platforms available, including Amazon's Kindle Direct Publishing program and Draft2Digital, among others. Many people are eager to become published authors, and it's now become much more common for someone to publish.

But a published book doesn't mean success. It isn't like a business card if no one bothers to read it. The average self-published book earns around $500 within an entire year. Don't let that be you.

The only way to avoid this fate is to become familiar with the industry beforehand.

The first thing you should do before writing a book is determine how long it will take to write the book in its entirety. Have you ever heard about the concept of things taking as much time as you allow them to? You want to gauge how long your book should take you to write because you want to build momentum.

Having momentum, especially if it's your first book, will enable you to progress with your writing while life takes place. When you have no timeframe or completion date in mind, it's easier to make writing your book an ongoing project.

If you don't have a deadline in mind, your writing process can go on for several months. This will make the entire writing process more stressful than it needs to be.

But if you decide you're going to finish your book within a set time period, your level of commitment and focus will be greater, giving you the momentum you need to get the work done. And what if you don't complete your book in the set time—let's say three months? Chances are you'll still be closer to your goal than if you started writing without a timeline in mind.

Again, having a set timeframe in mind is imperative, because it propels you to take action. And because you know this isn't an ongoing thing, you're more inclined to put your butt in the chair and get it done.

To help you write faster, first decide how many pages you want to write each day. For example, if your goal is to write 5,000 words a week, that's 1,000 written words daily Monday through Friday. 1,000 words is equal to about four printed pages.

If 1,000 words takes you about an hour to write, you'll automatically know that you have five hours to commit to writing each week. Commit to working within the container of a set timeframe, and it will get you closer to your goal of a finished book faster.

After you've picked a timeframe for writing your book, choose to stick to a schedule. Let's say you're writing a 20,000-word book. If you write 5,000 words a week, you'll have your book completed in one month's time. If you are writing a 40,000-word novel, you'll finish in eight weeks' time, and so on.

The second thing you will need to do before writing your book is become familiar with books within your sub-genre.

The reason I didn't say *genre* is because this is a bigger category. Your sub-genre falls within the broader genre.

It's the sub-genre within the genre that you need to look at. Why? Because here you'll be able to pinpoint what it is your target reader wants in a book.

For example, romance is a genre. Is it smart to say you're writing a romance book? No. Why? Because if you were to look at the romance genre on Amazon's website, you'll see that there are a number of sub-genres under the romance umbrella, including contemporary romance, African-American romance, multicultural romance, clean romance, and so on.

You'll want to hone in and read at least two top-selling books within a sub-genre you're interested in writing in. Also, read the blurbs of a few books. By doing so, you'll notice common themes popping up and you'll get a sense of the tropes readers are *expecting* when they open up one of these books.

Blurbs will clearly show you common themes that you'll have to keep in mind as you write your book. You'll also notice certain keywords while reading them. In addition, observe how books in your sub-genre are packaged. Learning about your sub-genre will be part of your reader analysis.

You don't want to write a book, and only after your book's written start thinking about the potential readers of that book.

Passion projects that don't give thought to the end-user's experience—in this case, your readers—don't often get read. Observe what your target reader views as a valuable use of his or her time, and give them more of what they find valuable.

Knowing who your ideal readers are beforehand will give you more confidence when you're writing your book, so look at what books are already being consumed.

Third, what is your purpose for writing your book?

Before you write, you should know your end goal. Even if writing a book has been your lifelong dream, how will your book serve readers?

**If you think about the purpose of your book beforehand, you can come up with a plan.**

Your plan may be to establish your expertise with your book so potential clients can see that you're knowledgeable about your subject. Maybe you want to use your book as brand collateral, and your goal is to print a workbook that your clients can use to organize their business. Or maybe you're writing a book to launch your speaking career.

If fiction's your jam, you might be writing your book because you want to write an entire series and create some passive income. Regardless, knowing your purpose—the reason you're going to spend time writing a book—is important because it'll be part of your self-publishing roadmap. In one sentence, you should be able to define your purpose for writing your book.

# The Foundation

# CHAPTER 5

# USE SYSTEMS TO WRITE FASTER

A couple years ago, the standard belief was that it takes one whole year to write a book.

Why?

The first reason is because publishers took at least one year to publish a book, sometimes longer, and rarely less. The second reason is because writing was viewed as an 'in addition to' part of an author's life—in addition to her day job, in addition to her marriage and household duties, in addition to being a mother. Because writers also have to live their day-to-day lives.

'Life' meant he had to squeeze in time after going to a nine-to-five job, taking the kids to their after-school activities, and maybe even watching a movie. Everything takes time, and the writing was often low among a list of priorities.

But the self-publishing industry and indie authors blew those preconceived notions out the window. At first, a handful of authors published three and four novels or nonfiction books a year, and then they shared their processes in online forums with other authors. This wasn't a book publisher talking—it was their *peers* speaking directly to them.

Many decided to try the techniques they were hearing about. Why? Because as self-published authors gained more power to shape their careers than ever before, the difference between being able to publish one book versus two books a year could prove significant to their bottom line.

Occasionally, there were some authors who wanted faster output because readers couldn't wait for the next book.

Authors became more efficient and talked about systems, schedules, and tools that made the writing process easier. There was Scrivener to help with organizing research and other notes, there was Freedom to block the internet and Facebook temptations, and there were apps to add background noise to help their concentration.

## Let's Talk It Out

I remember a twenty-plus page thread on a popular writers' forum called Kboards. The wife of a military man was sharing how a piece of software had completely revamped her writing schedule, making her more efficient at self-publishing. She'd gotten so much faster at writing her books and couldn't wait to share.

The software she was referring to was called Dragon Naturally Speaking.

It was a game-changer for her, and for the many indie authors who read the thread and tried the software for ourselves. The software freed authors from having to sit behind a desk, typing away. Instead, we could sit at our desk and talk aloud. We could even bypass the desk and computer altogether, instead talking into a recorder.

But why did authors choose to talk instead of write out their words? Because the average human being talks at a rate of 110 to 150 words per minute. Let's say it takes you one hour to type 1,000 words, or four pages. Think about if you were to speak instead. In theory, you could "talk" out those 1,000 words in under fifteen minutes.

Unlike casual speech, as you dictate your book you will probably go at a slower rate. After all, you're thinking as you choose your words, and this slows things down a bit. But in my own experience, I went from taking one hour to write four pages to just fifteen minutes. Yes, the time spent writing decreased to one-fourth of what it was before I used the software.

Imagine, there was a time I also used to write something out on paper before typing it onto my desktop. Talk about major time suck.

But I want you to grasp how amazing this is for you, as someone writing a book. If your goal is to write 1,000 words daily Monday through Friday, your writing for the day can be achieved in under twenty minutes, depending on how fast you talk. Or you can take a full half an hour to write, and the other half hour to edit.

It's simple math, and it'll work in your favor because software such as Dragon Naturally Speaking allows authors to reach their goal at a faster pace. At 1,000 words daily, you can write 5,000 words in one week. That's 20,000 words within just one month. If you are writing a 40,000-word novel or a nonfiction book, it could be done in two months.

You can be eight weeks away from your first book.

Increase your word count from 1,000 words to 2,000 words, and you'll complete a 40,000-word book in one month. Technology has allowed us as creative beings to cut through the excuses. Because now you have reason to talk it out.

If you're a perfectionist, or writing makes you feel stressed out, by choosing to talk—especially if you use a recorder with a USB port that can be inserted into your computer afterward for transcription—you may feel the words come more easily to you when talking.

Think of your ideal reader as someone who wants to *hear* from you, because they do. Dictation may also allow you to get into a flow state more easily.

Initially, you do have to train the software to understand your accent, and you may want to use common names if it doesn't understand uncommon names, then replace them later on. This software can be downloaded instantly from Amazon, or you can buy it on a disk.

But there are many other options out there. If you're interested in a lower-cost option, Google Chromebook comes with a voice typing feature on its menu bar, under Tools. In addition, iPhones have dictation software.

You can also download software in the Google Play store, such as Otter. However, I'm only personally familiar with Dragon Naturally Speaking and Google's voice typing feature on the Chromebook.

Being able to write your book while washing dishes at the sink, going on your evening walk, or driving in your car are all perks of this type of "writing." Many authors are choosing dictation to write their novels.

And today, dictation is even more convenient for people who want to become authors.

You can also record your voice on your phone or in a recorder and send it to be transcribed. Of course, you'll have to edit it afterward, but this will also save you time.

Companies like Rev.com offer transcription for $1 per recorded minute. There is also online software, such as Temi.com, that lets you upload your recording and it'll do the transcribing for you for $0.10 per minute.

Some options will be more accurate than others. For example, Rev will be more accurate because real humans transcribe your work. However, if you don't mind correcting some errors, you may want to go with a lower-cost option.

## Time Blocking

Besides dictation software, you might want to time-block when writing your book. Don't just sit at your desk and begin working. Give yourself a time limit. The Pomodoro Technique is used by authors to incentivize them to get the words out. While Pomodoros are traditionally 25 minutes, you may want to opt for 15-minute, 30-minute, or 1-hour sprints instead.

Having a timer running and knowing it'll run out helps to propel many people into action. You know that the time is short to create words, and you don't want it to end having produced little.

Which brings me to my next point: when writing, don't edit. Writing and editing require different parts of the brain. The writing part is when your creative hat is on in full effect, and the editing part is when the critical hat is on.

*You don't want a critic looking over your work as you're creating.*

Absolutely don't self-edit as you're writing. Instead, either edit the chapter after it's done before moving on to write the next chapter. Or edit the book after all the chapter are written.

Good books aren't written in the first round.

Every book needs to be edited for a reason. Take that as a source of comfort. The most important thing is that you've written.

## Tracking Spreadsheets

Whether you type your words or dictate it, another component you can add to your system is tracking spreadsheets.

Many prolific authors use tracking spreadsheets to help them stay on tasks with their word counts.

Using a spreadsheet system, they record their daily, weekly, and monthly word counts.

If you're a visual learner, tracking your output like this can greatly increase your pace. It'll enable you to see your progress and when you've updated your word count after you've finished another writing session, you'll both feel good about your progress and continue to build up momentum.

As we wrap up this chapter, you now know that writing a book has become a much easier process than it used to be. Gone are the days of notebooks and typewriters (well, unless you prefer them—some do).

If you choose, your laptop can play less of a part in your writing process. Because what's easier than simply talking to create a book that can impact many lives?

You now have even less reason not to self-publish your book. If you weren't before, today is the day to get serious about your goal.

# CHAPTER 6

# WRITING BEATS

In this chapter, I'm going to talk to you about getting the outline of your book onto the page.

Many people want to write, but they don't know how to organize their thoughts. They put plenty of pressure on themselves, and so their thoughts remain trapped inside their heads.

But it doesn't have to be this way.

Outlining a book is meant to make your overall writing process easier. Why? Because it acts like a roadmap, giving you directions as to where to go next. So in outlining, writing the main point of each chapter and then breaking down what happens in each chapter is your roadmap for proceeding to the next logical thing (or chapter).

You don't want to just start writing. If you're writing nonfiction, maybe you had to conduct extensive research on your topic. Or maybe your book will be based on your own experiences. Regardless, being able to clearly identify the main points in your book is imperative to success.

Why?

Well, if you can't clearly map out your book in some sort of logical format, it doesn't factor in well toward your bigger goal of writing the book in its entirety. Having some structure beforehand shows that you know what direction you're going in, which will enable readers to trust you as their guide. A confused writer means a confused reader, and chances are he or she will not make it to the end of your book.

But what if you don't want to write a formal outline where you list the chapter numbers, the subject of each chapter, the subtopics of each chapter, and so on? What if you want a quicker version? Here's the good thing: there are many successful authors who don't use an outline. Instead, they use a looser format called beats.

A beat is a unit, or one to two sentences describing the main point of a chapter. It's what happens within your chapter. A chapter would have at least three beats, and you as a writer would link the beats together with what happens in between each beat. This will make up your chapter.

So if you were outlining using beats, on one page you'd write down at least three beats—this is what happens first, this is what happens next, etc.—in chronological order. Then you would move onto the next chapter and follow the same process of writing down the units, or beats, of that chapter.

For example, if you were writing a book about the benefits of exercise and your opening chapter shared your own personal experience, you may have written down these three beats: I was feeling down and out and would eat ice cream every day after dinner. I weighed myself on the scale at the gym and was at my heaviest. Then I moved a pair of jeans that I'd never worn from the back of my closet to the front as a reminder of my weight loss goal.

In this one opening chapter, we know that three major things happened. First, the author had ice cream daily. We also know something led her to go to the gym. And we know she felt motivated enough to hang a pair of jeans she'd bought at some point in her life at the front of the closet as motivation toward her weight loss goal.

Now, if you were this author, all you have to do is tell us what happened, whether it was internal or external, that made you want to go to the gym in the first place. What kind of commitment did you think it would take? Fill in what happens between each unit.

And as you link the beats in a logical order and the chapter wraps up, you'll share what else happened for you to feel committed to making a change by hanging those jeans up in front of the closet as a daily reminder to get fit.

When you connect the beats, you'll have created the narrative or scenes that make up the chapters of your book.

Whether you use events, dialogue tags, scenarios, or facts to form your beats, once they're written down, you'll have a mechanism to connect the dots. Filling in what happens in between each beat will help guide your writing.

Just as we naturally use beats to link our main points together when we talk, you can use the same technique in your writing to move your book toward its conclusion.

# CHAPTER 7

## CONSISTENCY

If there's one factor separating writers whose books pile up in a draw from writers who become published authors, it's consistency.

In order for you to finish your book, you must consistently write it until you get to the end.

Nothing affects the writing process like a lack of consistency. It will affect your momentum, your ability to produce words and press on if you had a bad writing day, and your enthusiasm for your book.

The thing is, you should not write about what you're not enthusiastic about to begin with, because you'll have to plow through, and readers will pick up on that.

You can be writing about a topic a certain demographic might find boring, like calculus, but if you have enthusiasm about your project, not only will your writing process be easier, but you're more likely to find people who want to read what you have to share.

The thing about writing a book is that you have to be able to build momentum, and it'll be hard to do so if you don't have some level of consistency while you're writing. Stopping and starting is not the way to go. By now we know that writing a book is not something that has to take a whole year.

Many people are writing books in a matter of weeks because they have a system in place, and they're consistent with it. When you're consistent, you can make a note to yourself that there's a section of your book to be fixed, and go back to it the next week with a solution.

Your brain will keep the issue on the back-burner, so in the midst of plowing along with your writing, the solution will come suddenly. However, the solution may not have come to you if you'd stopped your writing altogether for a couple months.

Life is something we're all living. Think of it this way: you're writing your book for a set period of time. And within this container of time, consistency is an absolute must in order to finish your book.

Another reason why consistency is so important is that it'll help you build on your ideas more efficiently. Let's say you take off completely on the weekends to recharge, or for family time. On Monday, the last chapter you wrote will still be fresh enough in your brain for you to pick up where you left off. Writing consistently helps you develop a rhythm.

It's easy to solve problems as you're writing when you're consistent, because your book is the focus. But if you're writing sporadically, it's very hard to feel enthusiastic about your project and get into any state of flow where the writing just seems to come easily.

Inconsistency hinders your process. Do not let this be you. If you've had a habit of starting and stopping in the past, jump off this path and walk the consistency road.

Inconsistency will get you nowhere.

Be consistent and strategic with your writing. Whether you want to finish your book in one month or three, you must be consistent. And here's the most important fact.

If you're consistent, you don't have to put in a huge heroic effort. You don't have to write 2,000 words a day. No, you can aim for 500 words or 1,000 words, and once you're consistent, you'll get to your destination faster than you think.

Consistency allows you to do a little bit of writing each day, and the effort will snowball until you've completed the first draft of your book.

# CHAPTER 8

# TIME OF DAY AND LOCATION

One thing that you should take a look at when writing your book is how your consistency may be affected by various factors, such as the time of day when you write.

Perhaps you cannot sit and write leisurely at a coffee shop whenever you want. That idea is a fantasy for many people writing their first book. The kids need to be dropped off at school, breakfast needs to be made, or there's a train to catch. Or maybe meetings often run into your lunch hour, or you're in school and have classes in the evenings. Everyone's daily schedule is different.

You will have to figure out the best time of day for you to write.

Everything requires a sacrifice, so if your days are jam packed, you're going to have to make some adjustments.

These adjustments might include going to bed earlier than usual in order to wake up an hour before your household. Yes, I know that going to bed at 9 p.m. so you can wake up at 4 a.m. or 5 a.m. to get an hour of writing done doesn't sound like fun, but the time will pass anyway.

Either you'll have spent that time asleep in bed, or you'll have gotten your book done. Notice I didn't say go to bed at midnight and wake up at 5 a.m.

Lack of energy will not be helpful to you or give you the clarity of mind necessary to pour your ideas onto the page.

When you're looking at the best times to write, also consider your natural levels of energy. Energy management and taking care of yourself by doing things like exercising and eating healthy will benefit your writing.

Adequate sleep is important not only to your physical health, but also your mental health. There's nothing worse than waking up feeling groggy, and yet you have to dive into a mental task. We've all been there.

Decide on the best time of day for you. Is it the morning? If so, adjust your schedule to suit that. Or perhaps you want to write at lunchtime. You can pack your lunch in the morning to save time on running out to grab a meal. Have something already prepared, and you can maximize that lunch hour.

If the evening or nighttime work best for you, try to write during these hours as much as possible.

If you're able to experiment, I want you to try to write at different times and see which works best for you. Once you find your ideal time of day, put the pedal to the metal and get your work done.

Your ideal time of day or night might be determined by the amount of outside distractions, your energy levels, your work schedule, and so on. Pick a time when there's little excuse for you not to write so you can get your writing done.

There's another factor that affects you as a writer.

Location, location, location.

We often talk about how important location is for a storefront business. Before a business owner makes an investment, they must consider the location. After all, it will affect their bottom line, which is sales.

For you, your time is currency—it's an investment—and so you have to look at everything that affects your writing process, including where you sit to write.

Are you trying to write at home? What may take you one hour at the library might take three hours at home, thanks to distractions—your spouse keeps interrupting you, your dog wants some attention, your kids need homework help, your favorite show is about to come on.

Whether it's screen time or a family member, in this scenario, how fair are you being to both your writing and loved one?

Allocate quiet time for writing, even if it's a small block of thirty minutes a day.

And as you consider the time of day when you write, consider the location as well. Try writing at home, at a coffee shop, or at a library. Do try at least two different locations and at the end of the first week, see if it has affected your writing output.

If you know that writing at home isn't conducive to your productivity, then it's best for you to go to a coffee shop where you're not in such a comfortable environment where you might be tempted to sit on the couch, start your writing but then watch a bit of TV, or maybe start dozing off.

Perhaps you'll be energized in a space where other people are buzzing around, you can smell freshly baked pastries, and you can see others tapping away on laptops.

Your environment will affect your writing, and if you find that your usual location isn't conducive to optimizing your writing time, change your environment.

# *The Process*

# CHAPTER 9

# KNOW YOUR TARGET MARKET

I believe we all have a story to share, but you **have** to know who you're sharing your story with before you begin writing your book.

If you're writing fiction, your stories are either make believe or loosely based on real-life events. And if you're writing nonfiction, you'll likely weave in your own personal story or the stories of others through case studies.

Thousands of people self-publish each month, but guess what? Many books will go unread.

Some authors spend more money to get their books into the hands of readers than they will ever make from book sales.

Before you start writing, I want you to figure out if there's a market of readers out there for your book. There must be readers who have shown they want a book like the one you're writing.

How will you know this? There will be other books out there that are selling. By which I mean, if you were to scan the virtual bookshelves you would see several books in the category you're aiming for, with sales rankings preferably on the lower end. I'll discuss sales rankings more later on.

People sometimes think there are just three steps: write your book, publish your book, market your book.

If you're on a social media platform like Instagram, as I am, you'll see influencers tout making $5k in a month on a recently published book.

Guess what they never mention? Their large platform. It should be obvious that they have built-in sales because of their followers, and it'll be an uphill battle for those of us with smaller platforms.

Influencers have thousands of followers they're able to convert to readers. Their followers already know them, like them, and trust them, so buying their book is an easy decision.

But what to do if you don't have thousands of followers? Or you're not even on social media? Here's what you do. You go to a platform where there are thousands of people online in a buying mood, and they're looking for a book. Otherwise known as Amazon.

## Pick a Sub-genre

Websites like Amazon are a search engine. And to position your book to make sales, you want to pinpoint your book's category—also known as genre—and then its sub-genre.

You're basically scaling down to find the niche within the niche. Let's say you're shopping for a wig and only want a curly one, or you're purchasing a tennis racket and only want a Wilson brand. The wig would be the niche, and a curly wig would be a type of wig within that niche. The tennis racket would be the niche, and a Wilson would be the type of racket within that niche.

Make sense?

So instead of a real-life scenario, let's talk books.

Nonfiction is an overall genre, business and money is within that genre, but there are many sub-genres under this category including accounting, entrepreneurship and small business, investing, and so on. And guess what? If you were to click on investing, there are several sub-genres within this one category.

That's how far down you want to niche, because this is the audience you want to share your story with.

In a previous chapter, I shared why you want to narrow down your sub-genre before you write your book. Here, I'm going to emphasize again how important it is to know your sub-genre, because it affects many aspects of your process, including how you write your blurb.

You don't want to be a wandering *genre-ality*.

You want to start writing with your sub-genre already determined. Why? Because you absolutely should have a target audience of readers in mind. If you don't, then who are you writing for? Trying to speak to everybody within an umbrella genre will make your book too broad, and therefore unappealing to many.

By niching down and gaining clarity on your sub-genre, you'll be much more likely to hit the bull's eye with your sub-genre's tropes. Those readers will be happy, your sales will be happy, your bank account would be happy, and people in the wider umbrella genre will be more likely to find your book.

Why? Because sales equal visibility. And if you are hitting the tropes—otherwise known as motifs or clichés—of your specific genre, readers will be more likely to enjoy the book.

After all, they're expecting you to speak their language. They've come looking for a book within your sub-genre for a reason.

The longer you can sustain visibility in an online bookstore, the better your book will rank. This is when algorithms kick in and do the heavy lifting for you. Cool things will begin to happen, like the algorithm searching out other readers like the people who've read your book and sending them an email suggesting that they buy yours.

This is the Amazon recommendation engine kicking in.

Why would this happen? Because algorithms on book platforms want more sales, and they have information about the kinds of books their customers already enjoy.

Again, this can only happen if you're familiar with readers' expectations beforehand. In addition, you want to look at books within your sub-genre.

## Look at the Commonalities

Other factors to consider include the average chapter lengths of the books in the top 20. Are the chapters on the longer side? Or are they short and sweet? How many pages are in each chapter?

When you read reviews in your category, what are people commenting on?

Read a few, and you may spot gaps that your book can fill. When you read through the sample pages of a few books, how does the narrative begin—with dialogue, a story, a well-known fact?

Look at what types of books readers are already buying to inform your own writing process as an author. Of course you should write what you're genuinely enthusiastic about, but to increase your chances of success, research if there is a large enough market of readers available to read your book.

Read the sales pages. And actually read at least two or more books within your sub-genre. By doing this, you'll get a good grasp of common tropes, and what readers expect.

All of this research can be used not only in writing your own book, but in crafting your book title and subtitle as well. Earlier I mentioned that book platforms like Amazon are a search engine.

Bonus Tip: You'll want to utilize keywords in both your title and subtitle to optimize the chances of your target readers finding your book.

You can have an awesome book, but if your title or subtitle or series information (if you intend to write more than one book) don't indicate to readers that they've found what they're looking for, you've missed an opportunity.

Knowing your market means making it easier for your target audience to find you through your book title, cover design, and blurb.

## Gauge Readership Through the Book Rankings

When you write a good book and optimize your book's sales page, you increase your chances of visibility within a store.

When you're doing market research, look at how well books within the sub-genre you want to write in are doing. The lower the number, the more sales that book is achieving. For example, a book ranked #50 is selling way more books than one ranked #500, and a book ranked #500 is selling better than one ranked #50,000.

If the top books within your category all have low numbers, you're entering a more competitive sub-genre. At the same time, you don't want the top books in a sub-genre to be ranked #100,000 and higher, because this would mean sales are trickling in.

Do your research to determine which sub-genres you'd like to place your book in. On Amazon, you can place it in two sub-genres; you may want to pick one that's competitive as well as one that's semi-competitive. Regardless, place your book in appropriate categories, otherwise you'll have upset readers.

In the end, you want to place it where it makes sense and you can rank well, so that readers get a chance to see your book.

Sometimes it's better to rank higher in a less competitive sub-genre in order to increase your visibility. For example, there are millions of voracious romance writers. Does that mean you write a romance novel and place it in contemporary romance? Not if you don't know that niche's tropes.

Maybe your book is a clean romance, African-American romance, or multicultural romance. So you'd want to place your book in one of these smaller, less competitive categories. These are also all examples of smaller sub-genres that have large volumes of readers, but that are also less competitive than other sub-genres within the umbrella genre of romance.

**In the end, you want to research the market you want to write in, understand the expected tropes, and write an original book.**

By being informed beforehand, you'll begin writing your book with a clearer understanding of the type of book your ideal readers will enjoy.

# CHAPTER 10

# EDITING AND FORMATTING

## Editing

It's important that you proofread and edit your book before you hit the publish button.

You can proofread it yourself, or use online resources like Grammarly to check for errors. In today's competitive self-publishing climate, it's important that you set your best foot forward and give readers a good experience while reading your book. This will mean that you're presenting a product as error-free as possible when it comes to grammar and sentence structure.

You may also want to ensure that your chapters are not too long unless this is a genre norm. However, gone are the days of long 3,000-word and 4,000-word chapters. Shorter is *generally* better because of the shorter attention spans of today's consumers.

Our mobile devices, social media platforms like Facebook, and the rise of video consumption have made it easier for people to choose shorter options. They want to consume and move onto the next thing, so keep this in mind as you're structuring your book chapters.

As long as they can move through a chapter and feel satisfied that they're moving forward in your book, they'll be happy.

Don't write fluff in order to fill a word count. It's better that your book fulfill its goal without fluffy content, in addition to being free of grammatical errors, typos, factual errors, and so on.

If you plan to write your book and then hand it off to an editor, don't.

Instead, spend some time at least giving it one editing pass. You're going to find some errors, and there may even be parts of your book that you need to be clarified.

In addition, the more editing work a copy editor has to do, the more expensive your manuscript will be. This is why you, the author, should be your book's first editor.

If you can, read the first chapter of your manuscript out loud to hear those errors that our eyes can sometimes skip over. I say the first, because who has time to read an entire manuscript, but the first chapter will set the tone of your reader's experience.

Perhaps you might print out the pages and mark through with a red-ink pen, or use Track Changes as you review. Regardless, you do not want to send a completely unedited manuscript to a professional editor.

Before choosing an editor, you can request a sample edit. The usual minimum is 1,000 words done freely. This enables you to see how the editor works and if they're a good fit, and it also gives them a feel for the content they'll be editing.

Choose an editor that you feel will do a good job on your manuscript. In addition, one thing to note: just because one editor may be more expensive than another does not mean they'll necessarily do a better job. This has been my own experience. Choose an editor who fits your budget, who you feel will do a good job on your manuscript.

Keep in mind that an editor is not responsible for the success of your book. First and foremost, you have to create sellable content that readers will enjoy.

In doing your research, look at what type of editing you may need and the editor's past clients. Have they edited books similar to yours?

A reputable editor should have some sort of online presence, unless you're hiring a friend who's a teacher or something along those lines. But overall, you should be able to learn a few things about where they've worked and who they've worked with before you contact them.

## Formatting

An important aspect of your book will be its overall presentation. This includes the formatting and layout.

After your book's edited and you're looking at the interior layout, ask yourself if the text placement is easy on the eyes. Is the text reader-friendly?

Keep in mind, many readers will choose the eBook format of your book. That means readers should not see large chunks of text while scrolling down your page. This is hard for them to take in visually.

Have line breaks where appropriate. Include dialogue tags. Make key points stand out by leaving that sentence on its own. Understand that people are used to reading on a screen, and they do not want to see lines and lines of text.

Break it up for them so that they get the visual cues needed via the use of space to process what they're reading.

When your book's done, you can format your manuscript for yourself in Microsoft Word, then add the document into a book dashboard like Amazon KDP.

Next click on the preview button to see how the final version will look on a mobile device, tablet, or desktop computer. But this is easiest if your manuscript is simple text without other elements, like charts and pictures.

I've uploaded documents and the final layout looked good, but the file was a simple layout with a table of contents, clickable links, and the manuscript text itself.

You'll want to have a table of contents regardless of whether you're writing fiction or nonfiction, as readers want to be able to easily navigate through chapters on their mobile devices.

Alternatively, getting outside help with formatting your book is not expensive. You can hire a formatter on a site like Fiverr.com, or find someone with this skillset through a Google search. There are also free online tools that will format your Word document into MOBI or EPUB formats before you upload.

When a reader opens your self-published book, the quality of your finished product must match the quality of bigger publishers.

Today's publishing climate requires an increasing level of excellence from authors doing it themselves. Many readers are not able to tell who produced a book unless they look at the publishing details, and really, all they care about is their reading experience.

# *Your Book Presentation*

# CHAPTER 11

## COVER DESIGN

It's a complete myth that people don't judge a book by its cover. They certainly do.

If your book doesn't have an attractive cover, it will most likely be passed over (unless it's required reading in a classroom or book club).

Many potential readers will not even open your book if they're not drawn in by your cover. But why?

Because there are tons of other books to choose from when looking to buy or borrow.

I'm going to share some helpful tips that you should keep in mind when you're deciding on your book's cover.

**First, it must be genre specific.**

Please ensure that your book cover is informed by your genre. For example, a romance book might have a couple on the cover, or an attractive, shirtless male, or a sexy woman.

The litmus test is if you were to put your book on the virtual shelves next to other books. Would it fit in? If your book stands out in a bad way or doesn't fit the genre, it's not going to help your sales.

When you place your book cover on the virtual shelf of a book platform like Amazon, where there are thousands of potential readers, your cover design acts as a form of advertisement. The title, the colors used, the font type—all blend together to attract or repel.

Think about how your cover design will look scaled down. Why?

Because many readers will see it for the first time as a tiny thumbnail. The title and author name should be easy to read even at a glimpse.

Research book covers in your genre. Where do authors place their name—big and bold at the top, or near the bottom? What font type is most common? What colors are used often—yellow, green, red?

You are not imitating anyone else's design. Instead, you're being informed by what's already working within your genre.

In the end, you want your book cover to stand out, but aesthetically, it has to be placed in front of its ideal readers for maximum impact.

And there are many potential cover designers to choose from. Like editing, choose a designer based on your budget and their portfolio of work. Other factors may come into play, like how fast their turnaround time is, as some cover designers' schedules may be booked out weeks or months in advance.

A good thing would be to have your design idea in mind as you're wrapping up writing your book. You can then search for a cover designer as you're editing your manuscript.

Look at samples of their work. What appeals to you should appeal to readers in your market. Keep in mind that a cover will not help sell a book if the content inside isn't good.

Editing and cover design will work to sell a good book. I'll pause here to say that the author who writes a bestseller right out of the gate isn't common. For many of us, we've written at least one book before and learned from the process. That knowledge put us in a better place to examine the industry and how we can do better next time.

Nevertheless, you can write your first book and have solid sales that enable you to pay a couple more bills each month, book speaking engagements based on your book's topic, and so on, depending on your goals.

Having a great cover will get you closer to your objective of selling books. Designer prices range from $50 to $2,000. You can even find cheaper and more expensive options, depending on the designer.

You may want to save some money if there's a cover you really want, but don't neglect things like paying an important bill.

Basically, don't overspend when the self-publishing process can be done with low and moderate overhead costs. Get a great book cover within your budget.

# CHAPTER 12

## YOUR CONSTANT SALESPERSON

A blurb will act as the 24/7 salesperson for your book.

It's out there working while you sleep, while you're washing the dishes, and while you're eating breakfast. If you have a good blurb that entices a reader, along with a good cover, your book can sell itself.

The content of a blurb and how it's structured are important for your publishing success. You'll notice that the more successful authors begin their blurb with a hook or tagline. This will make a reader curious to know more.

**A blurb is not a book summary.**

Read blurbs in your category. What key concepts do authors mention, and are the same concepts mentioned in more than one blurb?

Your blurb is your book's pitch for readers to buy your book.

But here's the thing: many authors find blurbs hard to write, including me. The only thing to do in order to get better is to practice, practice, practice.

What concept, line of dialogue, or sentence can you write that will make for a gripping opening line? Think of it this way: your opening line acts a marketing tool that introduces the potential of your book to readers. The remaining sentences of the blurb reel in the hook.

Your first line should leave an open loop or question mark in readers' minds. As humans, we want to know the answer. **And if you've created a strong desire to know the outcome, get the help needed, or be entertained, they will buy your book.**

A blurb should also introduce a problem and convey the mood of your book. I encourage you to write your own blurb, even two or three versions of it, to gain practice in being able to describe your own book.

It will also help you pinpoint the voice of your blurb. You don't want to write a blurb with a light voice and short, quick sentences when your book is on a serious topic with high concepts, using a lot of jargon or long sentences.

Your blurb should be a reflection of your book. Your editor can help improve your blurb after you've written it. But if writing one isn't your thing, or you do not feel fully confident about it, you can also hire a blurb writer.

Once you're writing it yourself, aim for a minimum of 300 words. You're not writing an essay, but at the same time, you don't want to condense everything into one paragraph.

This will give you an opportunity to include a couple keywords relevant to your book. Keywords are important for search engine optimization, or SEO.

SEO will enable your book to show up higher in rankings, which will make it easier for readers to find you. Book algorithms will read these keywords and recommend your book via their search function according to the search phrases a person types in.

If you use helpful keywords in your blurb, readers will find you, and if your book sounds compelling, you'll likely see another sale. Having no keywords in a blurb can negatively affect your book because it diminishes visibility, despite any merits your book may have.

Overall, once a potential reader finds your book, you want to draw them in immediately. What will get them to buy? The cover, the blurb, and the reviews.

Reviews are something you as an author cannot control. But if you've written a good book, you'll get positive reviews. Statistically, not many people take the time to leave a review, so know that people who do leave them genuinely enjoyed reading your book if you got a positive rating.

As for any negative reviews, glean the nature of them, and if you find there is constructive criticism in those reviews, consider them lessons you can use toward producing a better book next time.

Do not respond to negative reviews. Readers don't want to see an author getting defensive about criticism. If you can tell that the person hasn't read the book or there are inaccuracies in a review, you can always contact the platform's customer support and file a dispute.

A blurb is part of your book's marketing.

Here are the key components of a blurb. First, have a tagline or hook to open the blurb. Second, highlight the best aspects of what the readers are about to uncover in your book.

Third, if your book is nonfiction, have lines or bullet points listing the benefits readers will get from reading your book. A fiction author might include lines that convey an emotion. And fourth, include the 'ask,' in that you ask readers to buy, read, scroll up, or some action word that encourages them to purchase your book.

The bottom line is you want to be able to describe your book in a compelling manner within the sentences of your blurb.

Yes, it's another step in your self-publishing process, but don't let it overwhelm you. After all, the book itself is done, and your blurb is simply the icing that makes someone want to bite into the cake.

# CHAPTER 13

# PUBLISHING PLATFORMS

Amazon is the biggest bookseller in the world. That includes Amazon US, Amazon UK, Amazon Germany, and Amazon India, among other countries.

Amazon is the platform that really cemented the self-publishing industry, so most authors choose to publish on their platform.

It is the world's most popular book search engine, and it has changed many writers' lives by helping them become published authors and by giving them access to readers. When you finally hit the publish button to distribute your book, your investment may yield you money to pay one bill or many bills, depending on how well you implement the information provided in this book.

For many authors, it took more than one book for them to gain momentum. But this scenario is mainly for those who want to become full-time authors who want to base their income solely on self-publishing.

However, if you want to publish a book as part of your larger business infrastructure, one book may be sufficient to gain momentum and attract other opportunities, whether as a consultant, influencer, speaker, podcast guest, or a featured interview in the media.

## Amazon: Kindle Direct Publishing (KDP) and CreateSpace

Uploading to Amazon's KDP dashboard is simple. The platform guides you with prompts that you fill in, much like forms at a doctor's office.

Amazon will lead you through a step-by-step process where you either type in your book's information, or select one of the options given.

Many authors choose to enter their first book into KDP's Kindle Unlimited program. Kindle Unlimited (KU) gives Amazon the right to be the only platform where your eBook appears.

However, the printed format of your book can be published elsewhere. While the eBook version needs to be exclusive, you can publish the first 10% of the content on another platform (such as your website) as a sample read.

Books are enrolled in the KU program for a period of 90 days, and then you have the option of keeping your book in the program or distributing it wide.

Kindle Unlimited allows Amazon's customers to read as many books as they want each month for a flat fee of

$9.99. Instead of buying your book, they can borrow it through this program. You as an author are then paid according to the number of pages read in your book.

Authors choose to stay in Kindle Unlimited because book sales and book borrows together weigh more heavily in Amazon's ecosystem. No one knows exactly how Amazon's algorithm works, but if you get a sufficient amount of buys and borrows, recommendations are then sent through Amazon's newsletter directly to the inboxes of other readers who may enjoy your book. The momentum gained from recommendations helps an author's sales.

If you want a printed version of your book, the option is located on the KDP dashboard. After you've uploaded your eBook and hit the submit button, Amazon will ask if you'd like to create the print format with them through CreateSpace, which allows authors to print books.

After creating a book through CreateSpace, you would then order a mock copy to check for any errors. Then, following any tweaks, you can approve the printed version online before publishing it.

## Barnes & Noble (B&N) and Apple Books

Another publishing platform is Barnes & Nobles. Though it's known for its physical stores, authors can upload their manuscript to B&N's platform and sell eBooks.

You can also distribute to Apple Books. This will allow you to gain access to readers with Apple devices.

So far, the three online platforms mentioned above are among the most popular for authors aiming to self-publish. Some authors choose wide distribution because they want to reach as many readers as possible rather than stay on the biggest platform, Amazon.

However, you could always enroll in Amazon's KU program for the initial three-month period and then pull your books, enabling them to be distributed widely. Through this process, you can weigh the pros and cons of having your book exclusively on Amazon's platform versus widely available on others.

The reason many authors choose exclusivity is because if your initial sales and borrows create a good amount of velocity and the recommendations to readers kick in, their purchases help your book's sales snowball. In some cases, authors find that the amount of sales on Amazon outweigh the benefits of their books being available elsewhere.

## Draft2Digital and Wide Distribution

Another option is to upload your book to the online platform Draft2Digital.

If you choose to upload your book to this platform, you do not have to upload your manuscript to B&N or Apple. Draft2Digital will distribute your books to these sellers for you.

Other platforms where they will distribute the book include Google Play, Kobo, OneDrive, and Baker & Taylor.

This means you won't have to do the work of uploading to multiple platforms, saving you time. Draft2Digital will also convert your Word document into EPUB format for eBook distribution. In addition, they can also format your manuscript into a paperback option for printing. The diverse options available to you as an author to upload your book and get your message out into the world are simply amazing.

Don't let this dynamic opportunity to share your story and directly profit from your work pass you.

# CHAPTER 14

# CONCLUSION

You now have a pathway to success as you self-publish your first (or next) book.

You know why it's important that you share your story. And you've learned seven steps to positioning your book for self-publishing sales, from why you shouldn't focus on editing your manuscript as you write your book to blurb strategies that impact sales.

The seven steps provided in this book are meant to act as a blueprint, but you still have to sit down and get it done. You've read this book, so I know that you're serious about pursuing your goal of writing a book. If, at any point as you're writing, you start to feel that your book has to be perfect, guess what? It won't be. There's no perfect book.

What's important is that you do your best writing.

Unmute your own voice and share what's inside your head.

Do not compare yourself to other writers. Instead, self-publish with purpose. In order to do this, you must remain clear on why you want to write your book and what message you want to share.

In closing, I want to encourage you to not procrastinate and put off writing your book. You can achieve your goal.

Now is the time to get started on your book and give your story a voice!

If you enjoyed this book, please leave a review.

## Let's stay in touch!

If you'd like to learn more about self-publishing, follow me on Instagram (@buildncreate) where I talk about sharing your story and making an impact.

www.ingramcontent.com/pod-product-compliance
Lightning Source LLC
Chambersburg PA
CBHW051356280526
45784CB00007B/2974